Professional Success – the Career Building Blueprint

by Arun Coumar

I0504466

Contents

Introduction

Choose a job you love and never work a day in your life.

- Unknown

I believe that people who are driven for success will find it building their best career.

According to a 2017 Gallup survey, 85% of the global workforce were not engaged in their jobs. A disengaged employee is distracted, inefficient, and interested only in how his job can satisfy his selfish interests. I have found myself in this category before. Being a disengaged employee leads to dissatisfaction and decreased impact on the job.

I have also worked in jobs where I was engaged. An engaged employee is focused, efficient, and aware of a greater company vision beyond herself. She is more likely to be satisfied and creating a bigger impact with their work.

I equate my best career with working in jobs where I am engaged. That means only 15% of the global workforce is achieving their highest levels of career success. My hope is that you read this book and find yourself inspired and equipped to join and grow that 15%.

Each of us will spend, on average, about 100,000 hours of our lives at work (50 hours per week, 50 weeks per year, 40 years). That is a lot of time wasted by disengaged employees. 85% of the workforce is not reaching its full potential.

What if each of those people dedicated that time to constantly seeking out the best possible job? In doing so, they would be building their ideal career.

As founder of Professional Success Coaching[1], I help my clients define, find, and win that job through creating their professional brand and guiding them through job searches. My clients leave with a mentality to seek out their ideal careers, to be constantly learning, growing, building, and having an impact. With this book, I hope to provide some of the basics that I give my coaching clients, which I have learned and developed through my personal career experiences as well as the past six years of informal and formal career coaching.

Though still early in my own career, I chose to write this book now because I am right in the middle of my pursuit for Professional Success[2], and the lessons I've learned so far can help other students and young professionals at what I see as a crucial point in their careers.

This book is primarily for graduating college students and young working professionals looking for direction in their careers. I've been there, looking for a direction to go as a college student and feeling lost, as if I didn't get that direction right early in my career. I have employed all the tactics described in this book with great success[3] as I chase maximum engagement, job satisfaction, and impact. I look forward to hearing how you have done the same.

This book is a blueprint for career building success. It is not one-time-use and does not promise fast results. This book contains a system for periodically reviewing and altering your career to maximize career satisfaction and impact.

---

[1] Learn more at findprofessionalsuccess.com
[2] Professional Success is defined in the first chapter.
[3] These tactics work just as well with many of my clients who are well established in their 30+ year careers

The concept of Professional Success is for people who describe themselves as "career-oriented" and "driven." Some people are content with treating their career as a steady paycheck. They are satisfied by that, and that is ok. You are providing for you and your family and contributing to the world. If you are satisfied with your career and have no intention to put forth the effort needed to make a change, this book is not for you right now.

About my Program

I started career coaching in college. I watched too many of my peers struggle through interviews at companies they did not care about, for jobs they were not really interested in. In many cases, those classmates settled for jobs that they were not excited about, only because they had not approached their job searches with intention and thought. I wanted to help.

I still want to help. I have since seen many of my colleagues suffering in their careers, knowing they want to get out but not knowing where they want to go or how to do it.

I am fascinated with career paths and figuring out what makes people successful. I spend a lot of time on LinkedIn, reading about and envisioning the career paths of seemingly successful people with big titles and colorful, established careers to understand the steps they took to reach the position they're in and how those steps contribute to the work they do now. I believe our careers should be looked at like a path that you build over time. This blueprint can be applied repeatedly to that path as you keep building it and progressing along it.

I designed my original career coaching program on a flight from Washington D.C. to San Francisco in May of 2018. The program consisted of one concept: Professional Success.

At the time of that flight, I was coming up on 1 year since graduating from Santa Clara University, and had settled into my full-time working life. I wanted to find a productive use of my free time and thought about something I had done during my time in college for younger students in my business fraternity:

"Tell me your dream job and I'll help you get it" was my "pledge task" for new members.

I conducted 63 sessions on this task in 2 years with the business fraternity. Through it, I learned and applied several skills for researching, networking, and succeeding in 63 unique job searches for my fellow students. I took away what those students valued in a dream job, and what they were looking to get out of college in terms of career progression.

My clients have since ranged from high school students to established executives and business owners, though I focused my program on college students and early-career professionals because I believe that's where people actively engage with career decisions the most, and can make dramatic changes to their career trajectory to maximize the satisfaction, impact, and engagement of their 100,000 hours.

I decided to package up the learning from my advising and coaching experiences to pass it on and help others achieve Professional Success on a larger scale. The result of that decision is this book.

What's your dream job? This book will help you get it.

You can learn more about my programs at findprofessionalsuccess.com.

Arun's Story

I arrived at college not knowing what I wanted to do. I took political science classes, thinking I would do a pre-law track because the TV shows about lawyers and law enforcement made the job seem cool. I fell asleep a couple of times in those classes. After my first year, I found myself jobless, frustrated, and uninspired, having put no action into my career development to that point in my life. I remember sitting on the couch in my parents' house during that first summer, yearning for a job. Any job. I dreamed of even going back to pizza delivery, where at least the Friday night shift was exciting, busy, challenging, and left me with a big pile of tips. I went crazy with nothing to do and would have been happy doing anything.

This experience taught me that drive, intention, and purposeful action in one's career is priceless when generating maximum career success. I went back to school the following year determined to figure out what I wanted to do, and then do it.

I transferred to the business school after one economics class got me interested. I declared my accounting major after the first day of introductory accounting class because the concepts made sense to me more than any other business subject. I attended every recruiting and professional development event that I could find and fit in my schedule. I visited LinkedIn daily to learn about the careers of people I met. I had a 3-inch-tall stack of business cards on my desk. I got involved in any way I could to build myself professionally. I was business fraternity treasurer, accounting association officer, club finance administrator, unpaid investment banking analyst, assistant to the Chief Investment Officer, and worked 15 hours per week at a bank an hour's commute from campus. I did my homework walking to and from the train station. I learned all that I could about careers in accounting. I knew what I liked from Friday night pizza delivery and these additional work experiences. I knew what I wanted to avoid from shadow days and talking to alumni. I found jobs offered to students and new graduates from my university that I thought I might want and made it my mission to get them.

In the three years from that first college summer until I graduated, I held 9 different jobs related to accounting, received over 20 job offers, and went to work for a specialist capital markets, technical accounting, and deals consulting group in a Big Four accounting firm – I had learned that I was fascinated with business deals, excited about the consulting lifestyle, and pretty good at accounting.

In the next two and a half years (bringing us to today) I redefined my Professional Success and I am taking steps to place myself on a path towards the new definition.

I found that accounting and capital markets deals consulting is not the perfect job for me. While I was excited by the work at first, that excitement wore off. I found myself getting more excited about leaving work at the end of the day than I was about arriving at work at the beginning, despite my best efforts in college to find the perfect job. I learned more about myself, what I loved, and what I wanted from my life. I moved cities twice, got married, threw myself into my lifelong hobby of cars, and discovered what exactly about my job interested and excited me - the deals, their strategy, and their effects.

I have learned that perfection is impossible. Work, at the end of the day, will always feel like work to some extent. Rather than give up and resign myself to a job where I am not engaged, this realization inspires me to persistently seek out the best-suited work for me to minimize and mitigate that "feeling of work." I follow the principles of this book every day in pursuit of maximum job satisfaction and work that will help me create my greatest impact on the world. This is my path toward Professional Success.

In the last 6 months, I have applied for and gotten into a top-10 global MBA program, launched a new career coaching business on the basis of the program I created in 2018, and started an automotive-focused strategy consulting firm. I left my job for the MBA and have already begun using my "future MBA" status to start discussions about part-time jobs and summer internships, along with starting my own businesses. These initiatives will give me the chance to do plenty of research to find the perfect next step for me, as I am on my own path towards my Professional Success: independent automotive strategy consulting.

On my path toward Professional Success, I am engaged, fulfilled, and satisfied, working to make an impact on the world. I cannot wait to see what the future holds.

This book is your blueprint to that path.

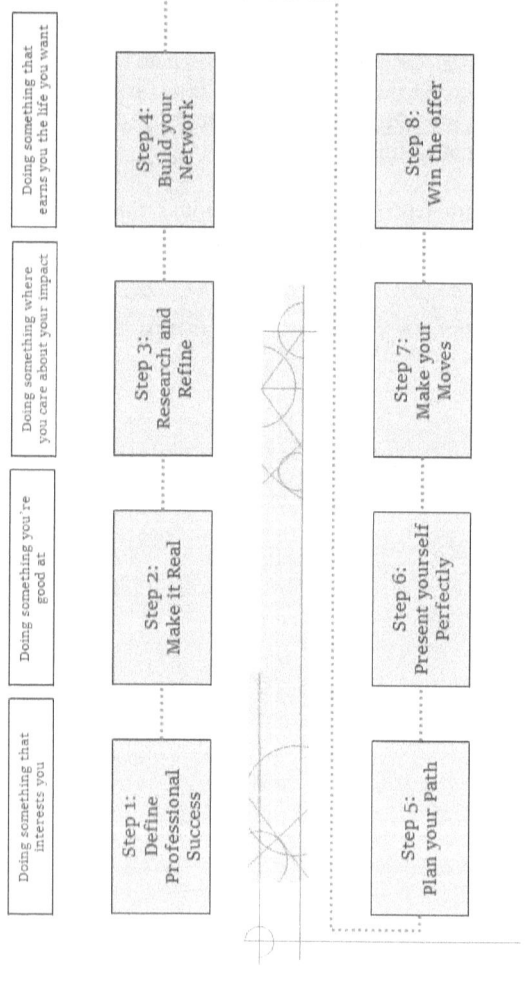

Part 1: Learn

Defining Professional Success

There comes a time when you ought to start doing what you want. Take a job that you love. You will jump out of bed in the morning. I think you are out of your mind if you keep taking jobs that you don't like because you think it will look good on your resume. Isn't that a little like saving up sex for your old age?

- Warren Buffett

Professional Success, as referred to in this book, is a career comprised of jobs in which you spend your workday:

1. doing something that interests you;
2. doing something you're good at;
3. doing something where you care about your impact; and
4. doing something that earns you the life you want.

If your job has all four of these characteristics, you will be fulfilled, satisfied, and engaged, while delivering your greatest impact to the world.

Professional Success is not necessarily getting paid 7 figures. It is not necessarily having a prestigious title. It is not necessarily being top ranked in your company. It is not necessarily being an entrepreneur. Professional Success could be any of these, but none of these generic examples fit into all four characteristics listed above.

Professional Success is personal and unique to everyone.

Professional Success is not something that you will define once and then hang up on the wall. You should revisit your definition of Professional Success regularly, to determine whether you are committing your working hours to a job aligned with your greatest impact and satisfaction. Over the course of your life, you will change, and your definition of Professional Success will change with you. My Professional Success looks very different now than it did 2.5 years ago. I got married, threw myself into the world of cars, and moved to London – my 21-year-old self could never have predicted that series of events when I was recruiting for full-time jobs in college.

Remember, **you will never completely reach Professional Success.** The satisfaction of reaching your goals will never last, and you will create new goals to chase. The pursuit of your goals gives you a reason to get out of bed every morning. **This pursuit is the only means by which you can deliver your greatest impact and derive maximum satisfaction.**

The next 4 chapters explain and exemplify, in detail, each characteristic of Professional Success.

Trait 1: Doing something that interests you

My dad is very interested in mental wellness. He is a trained psychotherapist who has worked for almost 30 years performing individual therapy sessions, hosting groups, teaching college-level courses, advising mental health companies, presenting corporate wellness courses, writing books, and directing a mental health clinic. In his free time, he reads books on mental wellness, practices his teachings in his own life, and works on improving the delivery of his business to his clients. He constantly has a long waitlist and is sought out for various opportunities because of his expertise in his field. His interest breeds his success - he is constantly learning and focused on his craft.

If you are interested in the subject matter of your job, you are likely to be more engaged at work. You want to learn more about your trade, you read about it outside of work, and you seek out new opportunities for more exposure to it, which is easy to do given your profession. Your interest leads you to be curious as you continue to learn and ask questions. Your attention span will likely be naturally longer. You are less likely to get distracted by a random text or news update. You will be more engaged.

Think about the following: What email lists do you subscribe to? Do you read certain topics of non-fiction books for pleasure? Do you watch a lot of YouTube videos or Netflix shows on a particular topic?

Author's Story: I am interested in strategic financial partnerships between companies. I subscribe to three daily business news emails with all the latest corporate deals and I am fascinated with understanding company strategy in the context of those deals. My first job out of college was part of the deals group in my company, where I worked on several joint ventures, mergers, and strategic investments. I was selected to help find business development opportunities for my group upon demonstrating my interest in deals. This interest in deals remained, despite my overall waning interest in the other areas of my job.

Trait 2: Doing something you're good at

I got to see firsthand proof that one of the partners I worked for in my accounting firm had risen up early in his career because he was simply good at the job. When I was an intern, I asked for help from this partner on a couple of occasions: once with a PowerPoint, and once with an Excel model. A partner's responsibility typically does not include helping interns with PowerPoints and Excel models, but I was naive and asked him anyway. I gave each deliverable my best effort as an intern, but I watched as he spent all of one minute reformatting the PowerPoint and giving me another capital markets law I had not thought to add in order to better make my point. I later watched as he quickly solved my formula error in excel. As a bonus, he proceeded to make a perfectly formatted summary tab without using the mouse. I aspired to be as good as this partner at the basics when it came time for me to teach interns. He not only was a wizard at computer tools, but also knew equity capital markets law like the back of his hand. I saw how his efficiency and commitment to knowledge must have contributed to his early career success.

The people who are most skilled at their job will likely contribute heavily to their employers and are therefore often highly rewarded. Raw skill is, of course, not the only trait required of good employees (I could refer you to any number of leadership and relationship development books), but it is ignorant to say that an amazing leader or relationship builder could be good at any job, regardless of technical skill required. If you are good at your job, you are likely to be more engaged and creating a greater impact.

Think about the following: What classes in school did you find easy? What aspects of jobs you have had were a breeze to get through?

Author's Story: I would make a terrible HR manager, lab technician, engineer, EMT, or account manager. I do not memorize the employee handbook of every company I work for; I struggled to understand biology in college; my math and computer science skills have only deteriorated since high school; I am afraid of having someone else's life in my hands; and am not a natural salesman. I have therefore steered well clear of those professions. Accounting, on the other hand, seemed to just "click" in my head. I was the annoying kid asking too many questions of the professor. I became the accounting class teaching assistant. I then worked for an accounting firm and specialized in advising companies on the most complex accounting matters they face. I defined myself as a specialist in accounting topics that most people in my group shied away from, enabling me to create a valuable brand for myself as a second-year associate.

Trait 3: Doing something where you care about your impact

To be truly successful, companies need to have a corporate mission that is bigger than making a profit.

- Marc Benioff

Every job exists to create some sort of value: profit and something bigger.

In my job as an automotive strategy consultant, I work with a visionary for the future of motorsport, the CEO and Founder of a company creating a racing series for electric production cars. In an introductory phone call with him, I heard his passion for energy sustainability and celebration of humanity's progress. I saw how this passion manifested itself in his company. The CEO is often sought out for media interviews and publications to cover his innovative company, and he found it very easy to speak at length about his vision. His belief in the impact his company could have is infectious. It is easy for this CEO to be satisfied with his job. He cares deeply about the impact that his company has as a platform for pushing forward through the world's sustainability agenda. As CEO, he must work to lead every area of the company towards success, so that his impact can come to fruition.

The value you provide in your job is in support of a greater impact. Do you care about that impact?

Your interests are finite and spread across a variety of distinct topics. They may shift or dwindle over time. Care, or passion, is persistent. It may be broad, or it may be very specific. What you are passionate about is what you could spend all day focused on without getting bored of it. Your attention span seems to know no end. Your first thought when you have free time is that you want to engage with your passion.

Do any topics or issues come to mind right now?

You will likely find initiatives, companies, or roles that are focused on your passion, and I will talk more about that search starting with Step 2. These organizations are working towards something you care about. It is their company vision or mission statement.

When you work in a job for long periods of time, you are guaranteed to have good and bad days. You will disagree with a coworker; you will get frustrated with a project. What I have found to be an important motivator in persisting with your work is thinking about the ultimate impact. That ultimate impact will help push you through any bad day at work, because you care about how your work affects the world.

Author's Story: My work involved helping companies ensure they are compliant with relevant accounting and financial reporting rules when announcing and reporting complex business transactions. I am interested in complex business transactions (a big merger, for example), and I am good at accounting. This interest and skill allowed me to excel in my work, as I accomplished the first two traits of Professional Success: Doing something that interested me and doing something I was good at.

However, I did not care about the impact that my work had in the world. Regulatory compliance in financial reporting is an extremely underappreciated, albeit necessary, job. Financial reports are read by investors and analysts, who make financial decisions surrounding the company. They often make several adjustments to the numbers in those reports to suit their analysis. What I spent most of my day working on was ensuring the numbers in those reports were as accurate and appropriately representative as possible. At all levels on my team, the end impact of our jobs was this same assurance to our clients. The end impact of my role as an accounting consultant felt quite small, and I never interacted with the people (investors and analysts) who appreciated my work, if they appreciated it at all.

Alternatively, I have loved cars since before I can remember. As a kid, every toy I played with was a car. I got my driver's license on my 16th birthday and unlocked a world of freedom, learning, and enjoyment. I care deeply about my own experience as a car owner and have invested a very large portion of my life to learning about cars, mechanics, performance, and racing over the past three years. This evolution of my passion solidifies my care for the impact of my work in this space.

As my work has begun to involve the automotive industry more and more, I have watched my own enthusiasm, efforts, and focus improve. I do extra research on the side, pursue side projects, and go the extra mile for my clients because I understand their business better than any other.

Trait 4: Doing something that earns you the life you want

You can have it all - really.

- Tim Ferriss

The first three traits of Professional Success are easy to achieve on their own. You could do something you are interested in, good at, and passionate about just by setting out to do it for yourself. However, at the end of the day, you need to put food on your own table.

The amount of money you make does not dictate your Professional Success. Professional Success is earning enough money for you to live the life you want.

Defining the life you want and determining what amount of money fits that life is a concept I learned from Tim Ferriss' *The Four Hour Workweek.* He describes the concept of Dreamlining, where you determine the monthly cost of the lifestyle you want (mortgage on a dream house, car payment, kid's tuition payment, travel) and work backwards (taxes, benefits) to determine your monthly required salary. Check out Tim's blog post on lifestyle design here[4]. My wife and I have done this in our own lives and it works brilliantly for making aspirational material desires seem smaller and more attainable. This is not a chance for you to answer the question "if you had infinite money, what would you buy?" Think big, but not so big that you envision yourself surpassing the richest of the rich. I will share my example of this trait in the following chapter, where you will also have the chance to design the life you want.

Earning the life you want is not as daunting as striving to become rich and live a lavish lifestyle. There is a wide range of monetary wealth that brings satisfaction to people. The life you want may be large at the start, but you will likely have to grow into it with time. **While on the path to Professional Success, do not focus on the money. Just make sure there is enough.** You will naturally grow your earnings as you progress through your career. Ensure your life aspirations fall within the range of what is possible at your level of experience and remember that you will have more to spend over time.

---

[4] tim.blog/lifestyle-costing

Author's note: Focus on the journey, not the destination

Your career will be long and full of failures and successes. In reading this book, I hope you will construct a planned career path ahead of you. The path will not be perfect after reading this book and employing its recommendations. **Professional Success represents a mentality: constant progress, seeking out the best for yourself, and pushing to create the best for the world.**

If you want more on this topic of financial planning, I recommend *Unshakeable* by Tony Robbins and the *Four Hour Workweek* by Tim Ferriss. You can find my story on this trait in Step 1.

Part 2 of this book provides tangible steps to build your career on which you can act immediately. The goal of these steps is to set you on a path towards Professional Success. They can be used repeatedly to keep pushing you further along the path. Keep them in the back of your mind and employ them when your Professional Success mentality deems it right to do so. Revisit Part 1 and Step 1 of this book when your Professional Success no longer motivates you. At the very least, I recommend once annually.

Part 2: Act

Step 1: Define Professional Success

All I ever wanted to be is who I am becoming.

- Unknown

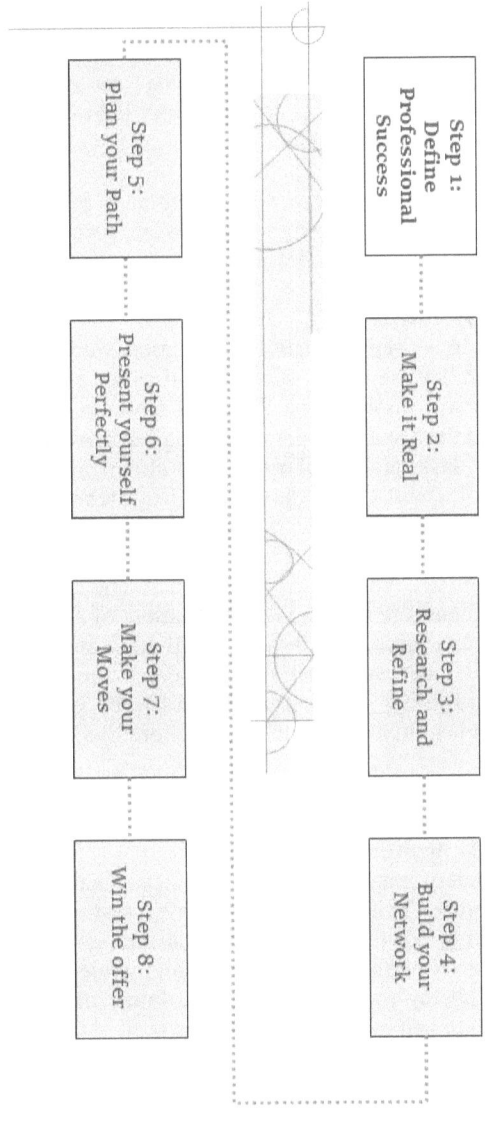

Step 1: Define Professional Success

Step 2: Make it Real

Step 3: Research and Refine

Step 4: Build your Network

Step 5: Plan your Path

Step 6: Present yourself Perfectly

Step 7: Make your Moves

Step 8: Win the offer

Below are some questions for you to answer. The answers will help you define your Professional Success. Try to answer on instinct rather than be influenced by others or overthink it. I recommend giving yourself sixty seconds to write down everything that comes to mind, and then stop. I have included my own answers below.

Question: What are your hobbies? What do you do with your free time for enjoyment? What sucks up your attention? What do you read and watch?

My answer:
Cars - Maintenance, modifications, driving, racing, tracks, traffic law, new cars, second-hand cars, car shows, garages, the future of mobility, the future of motorsport. I can (and have) spend days at a time doing nothing but driving. I love road trips, track days, and YouTube videos about racing, mechanics, and modification. I love the sound of a ratchet being turned and a Lamborghini V12. I love the smell of gasoline.

Initially, you will have more than one topic here. That is ok. My clients are able to list off a number of activities they do with their free time, and they can still hone in on and define their Professional Success through a combination of their answers, brainstorming, and research as described in Steps 2 and 3. The result is a final answer that looks more like mine.

Question: What are you really good at?

My answer:
Determining and defining the steps needed to reach a defined end goal. This book demonstrates that skill. I am good at breaking down a big future vision into several small steps that are clear and manageable. Therefore, while not suited to coming up with my own solutions to the future of mobility, I am well suited to helping others execute on their visions.

As an example, I completed my entire London Business School MBA application process in 1.5 months, while working full-time and moving to London. How? At the beginning of the process, I figured out what I needed to do to succeed and determined how I would go about accomplishing those tasks. The milestones I defined for the MBA application were:

1. Get 700+ on the GMAT;
2. Build a network of London Business School alumni and students to learn from and advocate for me; and
3. Complete my application, including nine long-form written responses.

Underneath each of these milestones was a list of tasks. Through systematically accomplishing each task in my step-by-step plan, I was able to complete all the milestones simultaneously. It certainly was not perfect – my friend got a higher score than me on the GMAT, several people I reached out to did not respond to me, and I argued with every single piece of feedback I got on my application essays. At the end of the day, however, I applied by the first round deadline and received an offer.

Question: What common issue do you get persistently angry about?

My answer:
Bad drivers. Poorly maintained cars. People who say they hate driving or they are terrible at driving. Uber drivers illegally parked on the side of the road and poor driving safety.

If people who didn't care about cars or driving had a solution that allowed them freedom from driving and car maintenance, the roads of the world would have less traffic, more freedom, fewer accidents, and less risk each time anyone gets behind the wheel. The future of mobility shift towards advanced safety features and self-driving cars is gaining momentum, but we still have a long way to go in most of the world to develop and implement a solution that serves these people. Finding that solution will motivate me to come into work every day and work hard. I will care about the impact of my work. I believe that the solution will benefit me, and billions of others.

Question: Imagine that you do not have to work to meet your needs. You can continue to work and make money to afford luxuries you want, but you do not need to in order to survive and have a reasonably comfortable life. For the sake of this question, imagine your age and life situation are the same as reality. How would you spend your time?

My answer:

1. I would leave my full-time job (at the accounting firm) and throw myself into self-employed income streams, giving me the freedom to work on the days and times that suit me best on projects I care about.
2. I would spend more time with my wife, doing the things we enjoy together.
3. I would travel more often to visit the people I care about, who are dispersed around the world due to multi-national parents.
4. I would go for drives. Road trips, mountain runs, night drives through big cities. Find the road less traveled, be outside in the daylight, use cars to explore the harder to reach places of the world.
5. I would get more involved in two areas of the car community: racing and aftermarket modification (car owners making performance and aesthetic improvements to their cars).

Picture the life that you described. This is your answer to "earn the life you want." For me, there are 3 clear points that make up "the life I want" from my earlier answers.

a. #1-3: Flexible working hours and creating my own projects
b. #2-3: Time and money to travel extensively and comfortably for the sake of people I care about
c. #4-5: Time and money to invest in my involvement with cars and the car community

For me, that is the ideal use of my time and the life I want. Point A gives me two traits to seek out in my jobs (flexible hours and creating my own projects), and points B and C are personal and fill the criteria for financially earning the life I want.

After going through this exercise, you may be thinking: "But my answers aren't all lined up in an arrow, pointing towards a single, obvious career…" That is ok. These answers are only to give you ideas. You are on the first step of the process. In Step 2, you will cast a wide net, and then do research to narrow it down. As you take in more information, your ideas and answers will become clearer.

After some research and reflection, eventually you will be able to come up with a single, cohesive definition that selects your answers that fit together into something that resembles a job. For now, notice whatever patterns you can find in your answers that look like they fit together to tell a story. Some examples are:

"I watch lots of cooking videos on YouTube. I am an avid runner, and good at teaching people how to make subtle changes in their lives for dramatic improvement. I get mad every time I hear someone say that they cannot eat healthy because it does not taste good. I want a life where I can afford a house with a nice kitchen and space for backyard workouts, I don't have to interact with people one on one, and I have time to spend going out with my friends in the evenings and on weekends."

- Potential corporate wellness program manager

"I love going on Zillow and looking at houses. I found myself fascinated by tracking house prices over time. I am good at making friends because I am very curious about other people and a good listener. I get angry when people make a blanket statement and blame all bankers for the Great Recession. I want a life where I can work hard 5 days a week to earn a good living. I like nice watches and/or jewelry and going out to eat often. I want my weekends free to be outdoors."

- Potential member of the Airbnb real estate team

To recap, my definition of Professional Success **at the time of this writing** is:

- Trait 4: Earn enough to travel and spend on cars while working flexible hours *(doing something that earns me the life I want)*
- Trait 3: Solving the future of mobility *(doing something where I care about my impact)*
- Trait 2: Using my skill of breaking down big visions into small steps and executing those steps *(doing something I'm good at)*
- Trait 1: Doing something involving cars *(doing something that interests me)*

What is your definition?

Author's note: Remember, you will likely never actually reach Professional Success.

There are two reasons for that:

First, your definition will change as your life progresses.

Second, your definition will change as you get closer to achieving it. We always want more.

Instead of having your eyes set stubbornly on that vision, form a path for your career that ends at Professional Success. The path will move you in the direction you want to go, even as that direction changes. Following this path gives you the greatest chance at satisfaction, engagement, impact, and earning.

You have some characteristics for your Professional Success. Now it is time to do some research, plan, and act. **This is not meant to be a strict process. Early action is better than a perfect plan.** You can always step backwards if needed.

Step 2: Make it Real

Do you know how great it felt that I knew where I was going? I was so relieved, because when you have a goal, when you have a vision, everything becomes easy. That is rule number one: have a vision.

- Arnold Schwarzenegger

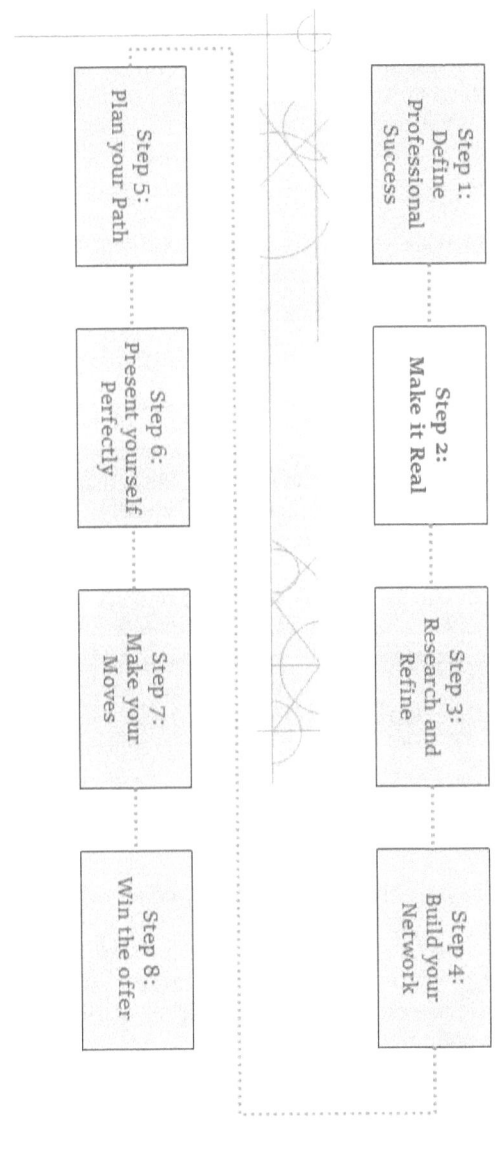

Step 1: Define Professional Success

Step 2: Make it Real

Step 3: Research and Refine

Step 4: Build your Network

Step 5: Plan your Path

Step 6: Present yourself Perfectly

Step 7: Make your Moves

Step 8: Win the offer

From the questions you answered in Step 1, you have a vague idea of a direction you want to go. It may not look like a job of any kind, but we will take additional actions in Step 2 that will formulate your current vision of Professional Success into a goal that you can work towards.

Convert your end goal into a first step

Take what you have learned about yourself from Step 1 and construct your ideal next job. It will have the following characteristics.

You are:

1. Earning enough to begin building the life you envisioned (i.e., not taking on more debt, beginning to invest in hobbies or priorities that will take time to build up, such as buying a house)
2. Using some of your time and money to engage in a hobby that you are interested in or passionate about, whether at work or outside of work
3. Working in a job that excites you on a regular basis because of your interest and/or passion
4. Skilled enough, or potentially skilled enough to be at the top of your field in your job
5. Setting yourself up with experience that is valuable for a future role

This is the bar you are setting for yourself for your next job.

Example: My first job out of college fit almost all these criteria:

1. I knew my job had good earning potential due to a fast promotion track and a higher starting salary than my other offers.
2. I knew that this earning potential would allow me to begin pursuing my passion for cars. I knew I would be working long hours but accepted that tradeoff for the earnings.

3. I was excited to work on deals that regularly made business headlines.
4. I had the potential to excel in my job as a consultant, solving complex accounting problems.
5. I wanted to make Partner in the accounting firm I went to work for. This is the highest title you can reach and means you are part of the leadership and ownership of the company. At the time, I believed that I was giving myself valuable experience for that future role (i.e., building up a series of promotions).

My job was part of an amazing first 2.5 years post-graduation from college. I have moved to London, gotten married, and bought and modified 5 cars (so far). I had the flexibility and means to dedicate time to my car passion. I was excited about the deals I got to work on because they frequently made headlines in business news. I was able to brand myself as an accounting specialist. The job contributed massively to my future success, including helping me qualify for one of the top MBA programs in the world. The MBA is my next step in the direction of my Professional Success.

I confirmed that while not a perfect fit, my first job met all those criteria I listed. As you evolve and grow, your current job may or may not follow you. Keep your self-awareness top of mind - what you once thought was your perfect job for life may not always stay that way, and this book gives you a blueprint for how to move forward from that state.

Research and self-awareness are two keys to optimally executing this blueprint. **You must avoid going into a job blindly. There is no reason to be surprised by the outcome of your career.** Step 3 will teach you how to do quality research.

Author's note: Research

How did I know all those things about my future job? It did not start at the beginning of college. It did not start after my summer internship with the firm. Not my parents, nor any other family members are in the accounting field. I entered college thinking I would get a pre-law degree because I had seen the TV show CSI (Crime Scene Investigation) and thought being in law enforcement looked like a cool job. My parents wanted me to go into medicine.

I built the knowledge I graduated with through extensive research. I selected my first job out of college based on this knowledge. Learn more about the research tactics in Step 3.

Make a list

Make a list answering the following question: given the characteristics of earning, hobby, passion, skill, and experience, along with my answers to the questions in Step 1, what first career step could I take in the direction of Professional Success? What does that job look like? Make a long list. The list does not have to be specific job titles at specific companies but should have some general descriptors for a role or company.

Some examples are: "I will work with horses on a farm (you're interested in horses and you enjoy manual labor); I will work in air traffic control (you're passionate about airplanes and get angry about flight delays); I will work for Ford's marketing department (you respect the company, you're passionate about cars, and you are interested in advertising); I will work in Airbnb's real estate team (you're interested in real estate and care about creating responsible real estate finance); I will create corporate wellness programs (you want to work for yourself, you love cooking, and you want independence from individual clients).

Give yourself lots of options that you think may be a potential path. Think about all the possible activities that could fill your day, all the industries you could work in, and all the companies you respect. It will not be long before you are able to narrow these down.

Each line on your list is referred to as a "potential path" in the following chapters.

The next chapter describes how to narrow down the list.

Step 3: Research and Refine

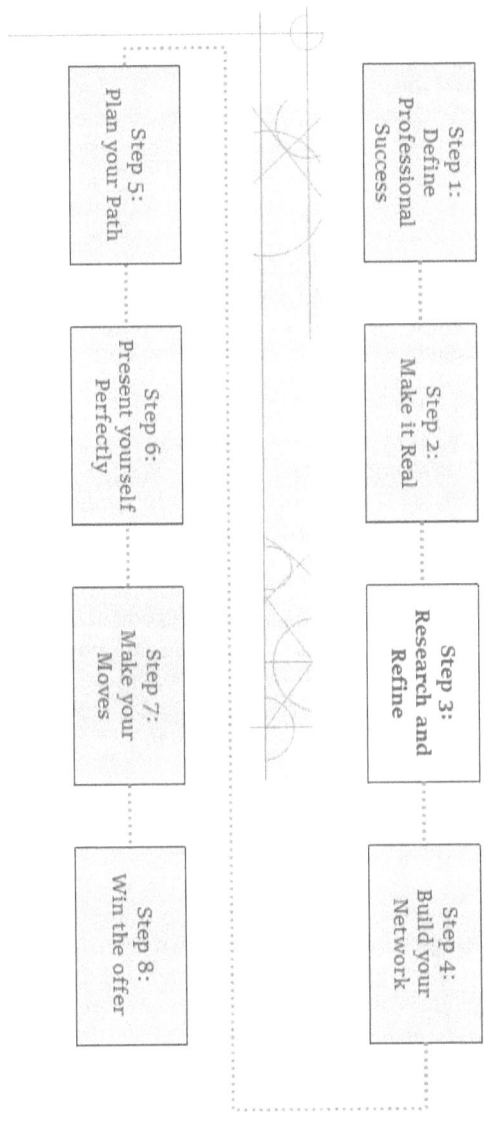

Step 1: Define Professional Success

Step 2: Make it Real

Step 3: Research and Refine

Step 4: Build your Network

Step 5: Plan your Path

Step 6: Present yourself Perfectly

Step 7: Make your Moves

Step 8: Win the offer

Now that you have your list, it is time to find out which potential path is the right fit for your first step towards Professional Success. How do you find out? Research. Your initial research can be done 100% from your computer and phone. I spent much of my sophomore year of college looking out my dorm room window, sitting at my desk, on the phone, writing emails, searching LinkedIn, and browsing company websites.

There are several means of research available:

Google: basic company and industry information
- Google "companies in the automotive industry in Seattle" to see what opportunities are available to you in your target industry in your location.
- Google "jobs in the horse industry" to get a better idea of what options are available to you for preexisting jobs in your target industry.
- Google "how to become a VR product manager" to understand what skills and experience you need to get into the field of virtual reality. There might be forum or blog posts, articles, or job postings you can look at to understand what is needed from you.
- Let Google be your first filter. If a potential path still excites you after browsing Google results or reading an article on what it takes to succeed in an industry, then proceed to the company website.

If you find yourself not excited about any of your potential paths after this stage, revisit Step 1. Pull out more answers. Think about whether your list is omitting anything.

After each research option, refine your list. Cross off or edit potential paths. Perhaps "I will work in the marketing department for Ford" becomes "I will work in automotive advertising," or "I will work on a farm with horses" becomes "I will work for Cavalor" (I googled "horse feed companies" and clicked on the second link).

Company websites: job descriptions and mission statements
- Find your target company's website. Go on their careers page and see what roles are available and what

those roles require. Are any of those roles a good fit for your definition of Professional Success? Learn about the benefits the company is offering its employees.

- Read the "about the company" page, learn about the company values and culture. Understand the company's mission statement. Do you agree with it? Does it inspire you? Do you care about it? Learn about the management of the company - do you think you could work for them? What are their backgrounds?

Glassdoor: salaries and reviews

- Glassdoor has crowdsourced data on every sizable company out there. You will likely be able to find salary data to have an indicator of your compensation, helping you understand your earning potential for your potential path.
- The website also has reviews of companies from employees. These will help you get a better idea of what the culture and working environment would feel like for you on your potential path. Look for how many hours you are expected to work, training resources, and tone from leadership. Do these expectations match your vision for a potential path?
- Look for red flags. Glassdoor provides salary information that is fairly accurate, within five thousand dollars, in my experience. From your Dreamlining exercise, work out how much money you are willing to accept from a first job (consider your living situation, other fixed expenses, and what hobbies you want to pursue). This is your chance to eliminate potential paths that will not pay you a living wage or represent a giant pay cut.
- If employee reviews are consistently bad, walk away. One or two negative reviews is normal of any reviews page, but consistent negativity is a red flag. Take all reviews with a grain of salt and get a feel for the job satisfaction of the employees.

Revisit your list. You should have between 2-5 jobs left. You will have a better idea of your potential path, which will allow you to get more detailed with your research. You can now expand your research to include learning from other people and dissecting potential paths.

Step 4: Build your Network

I've come to believe that connecting is one of the most important business— and life—skill sets you'll ever learn. Why? Because, flat out, people do business with people they know and like. Careers—in every imaginable field— work the same.

- Keith Ferrazi, author of Never Eat Alone

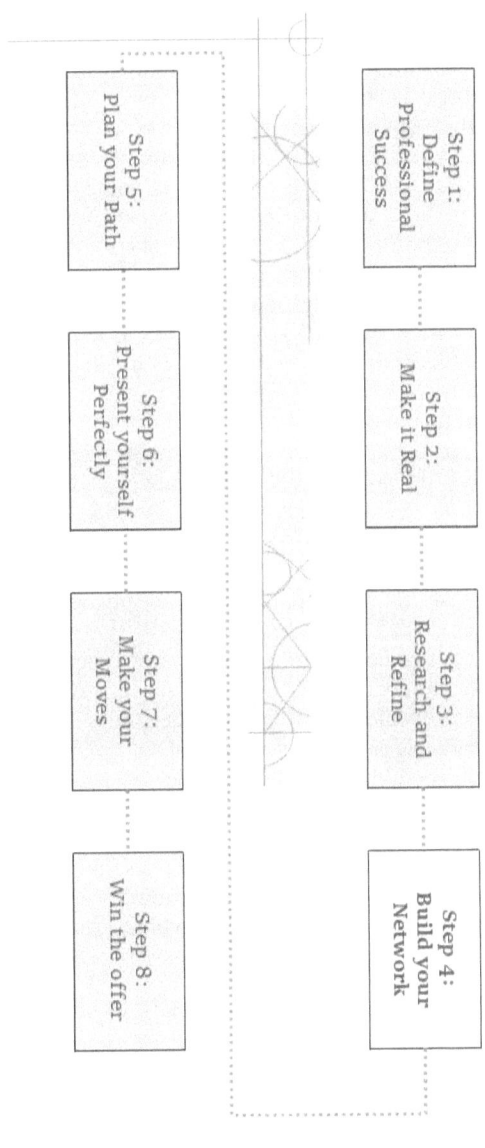

Your network is your best resource when it comes to doing research and finding a new job. Your network will be made up of people you know and people you will meet through your job search process. It will grow over the course of your job search, and you may not even know the person who will be your best reference yet. During this research phase, conducting informational interviews is the most valuable use of your time. Going through the process of conducting informational interviews is how you will build your network during this step.

- An informational interview is a conversation, between 15 minutes and 1 hour in length. It will be prompted by you. You will use the time to explore someone else's job, company, or career to see if it lines up with a potential path.
- The exploration is an opportunity for you to learn all the unknowns about your newly shortened list - ask questions to which you cannot learn the answer from Google or Glassdoor.

You must first find people who you want to interview.

Below is a good procedure for sourcing people to speak with about your potential path. Some of these people will become connections, which I will reference again in Step 8. Connections are very valuable resources to accumulate.

- There may be some people already in your network who would be valuable to speak with. These people are already working at a company you are considering, in a role similar to the one you are considering, or in an industry that aligns with a potential path. They are your family, friends, classmates, ex-coworkers, and industry peers.
- After speaking with people already in your network, you may have some recommendations for new people to connect with. If you still want more information before further narrowing down your list, reach out to these people next.
- If you cannot find anyone in your network or you've already spoken to everyone you know that could be

helpful, take your search to LinkedIn to find people who may be able to help shed some light on your potential paths. Look ahead to the LinkedIn chapter to learn more about how to focus and execute your search.

Author's note: The Request

Your request for an informational interview will sound something like:

"Hello, I am really interested in [insert your field] and eager to make an impact as I [change careers/enter the workforce]. I am trying to learn as much as possible about [your field] now in order to be best prepared and ensure my efforts are being directed appropriately. Would you be free for a 30-minute chat about your role, your experience, and your background?"

Tailor your request to the appropriate level of formality depending on who you are talking to. Generally, the above example contains the right amount of information to address the questions of anyone in any of the three groups (network, recommendations, strangers) as to who you are and why you are reaching out.

Send the request through email, text, or LinkedIn. However you can get a message to him.

There is likely someone out there (who you will hopefully find during this informational interview process) doing work that looks very similar to your definition of Professional Success, or who has taken a few more steps down your potential path. Make her a priority.

What you are looking to gain out of informational interviews, more specifically than learning more about the individual and her story is:

- What is her education background and does it matter for her current job?
- What was her first job? How has her career evolved?
- How did she execute each job change if she has changed jobs?

- How long has she stayed in each job she has held?
- How has her experience benefitted her, both working in their current job and initially securing their current job?
- Where does she see herself in five years? Is her role part of a long-term career or a short term stepping stone?
- What motivated her to take the job in the first place?
- What does her "day in the life" look like?
- Is she satisfied?

Regarding the company that the person works at, you should aim to learn the following:

- What is the company culture?
- What is the approach to hierarchy?
- How are the benefits?
- Are administrative tasks and meetings a big part of the job?
- How often does she hear from leadership?
- Is autonomy important and emphasized at all levels?

These pieces of information will tell you whether the company will enhance or stifle your ability to make an impact on things you care about and focus on things you are interested in.

In addition to these generic questions about their careers and employers, you should aim to learn more about his life to see if the job fits your entire definition of Professional Success, including earning you the life you want.

- Does he have a family?
- How many hours does he work each week on average?
- Nights and weekends?
- What does he do outside of work? How about his coworkers?

While on the subject of working hours, be careful not to give the impression that you will shy away from hard work. There are a number of career paths out there in which long hours are an assumed part of the job – ensure your question comes across as simple information gathering, as opposed to a filter for avoiding long-hour jobs. Ask the tough, honest questions about work-life balance of your friends and family who work in a similar role.

Finally, while you have already looked at Glassdoor and learned about salary estimates, if the conversation seems appropriate, bring up the topic of pay. In all my informational interviews, I can count the number of times on one hand that I have gotten specific salary numbers for a prospective job. If you feel it is appropriate, it is still good to get a general sense from an insider rather than rely solely on the internet.

Follow up with your contact over email after you have this initial chat with him, either later in the same day or the following morning. The message can be brief but should mention something personal about the conversation. The content of the follow up message must be in this order of priority:

- Gratitude
- Personalization
- Additional questions, suitably answered over email
- Request for further action, if any (referral, introduction, another conversation)

Regarding requests for further action, here is a general set of rules to follow. The request depends on who your conversation was with and should be based on the dynamics of each relationship. This guidance is just for consideration and is not necessarily appropriate in all situations:

- Peer (someone around your same level): job referral
- Superior (a manager or leader in the company): introduction to someone on their team
- Both: another conversation

Here is a follow up email I have written, about 8 hours after the informational interview (on a Friday). I had reached out on LinkedIn to learn more about a managing director's strategy consulting firm, and we met for coffee. I have changed the details for anonymity.

Taylor,

Great to chat with you today, I really appreciate you taking the time to meet. I got a good glimpse into what goes on at Consulting Partners and I am interested in staying in touch. I'm definitely interested in further exploring the possibility of a part-time internship with Consulting Partners during my MBA.

If you're open to it, would you be able to introduce me to one of your consultants or managers? I'd be interested in getting their perspective on Consulting Partners as well.

Hope you have a good weekend.

Best,
Arun

If you do not hear back from your contact, you should only follow up if you require a response to additional questions or a request for further action. Depending on the urgency of the request, you will need to determine what is an appropriate amount of time to leave before following up. In my case, Taylor responded on Monday evening. I would have followed up on Wednesday if I had not heard back. Never send your follow up email more than a week later. If I had needed to follow up, my email would have looked like this:

Taylor,

Hope you're doing well and had a good weekend.

I really appreciated our conversation last week, and I am continuing to think about what it would be like to work at Consulting Partners, after learning your perspective on the firm. If you can think of a couple of consultants or managers who would be good people to speak with to get another perspective, I'm happy to reach out to them if you provide their name.

Let me know - hope to hear from you soon.

Best,
Arun

This follow up is tailored to a level of formality on the high end of the spectrum and shows that I respect the time of the managing director of a 400-person consulting firm. I know someone at that level will appreciate directness and action-based requests.

Following up is tough - I have failed many times to get what I was asking for in a follow up email. Regardless, I will always do my best to be respectful, grateful, and personal with each informational interview I have done. Following up is an absolute necessity in order to get yourself on the path towards Professional Success.

If you want more information on building a network, I recommend reading Never Eat Alone, by Keith Ferrazi.

LinkedIn - a subchapter

Almost every month of my college career (and still regularly to this day) I exhausted my monthly search limit on LinkedIn. At any given time, I likely have 4 or 5 outstanding requests to people who I am interested in speaking with. In my experience, no more than 1 or 2 of those people will respond to me.

One of my college student clients said to me: "What really helped change my perspective was the activity of LinkedIn stalking people whose careers I admired. This helped me focus on long-term goals rather than just looking for a summer job. It also helped personify different roles/industries which often seem vague or idealized on paper."

LinkedIn is where many working adults and students put their professional lives on display for all the world to see. They put their accomplishments, document their climb up the corporate ladder, share their locations, and they might even summarize why they got fired, what inspired them to start their company, or why they love what they do. These are all answers to questions to be used in an informational interview. This information is invaluable when it comes to learning about your potential paths, defining your Professional Success, and maintaining a mentality of constant learning, building, and growing.

Maybe you found someone through your Google research, such as a member of company management. Look her up on LinkedIn. See what her career looks like. Where did she go to school? Did her major matter? What was her first job? How long did she stay at each company she has worked at? Did she get a graduate degree? Did she make lateral changes, geographic changes, take a demotion, or try self-employment? You can learn a lot about someone on LinkedIn. Depending on the field (this is the most true for businesspeople), you will find that many people are very proud to put up their career history in detail. Find people whose career paths interest you, and request to talk with them using the message on the next page.

Informational Interviews

As I mentioned earlier, LinkedIn works as a means of reaching out to someone whose career you want to learn more about. When I say, "reaching out," I mean send a connection request. **Include a note in the connection request.** You have 300 characters to make a solid case that opening a dialogue with you will be worthwhile. I use something like the following, which is a shorter version of the message used for initiating an informational interview which I suggested in Step 4:

Sandy - I am looking to move into consulting and believe Consulting Partners would be a good fit for me based on my extensive research and a company mission statement I believe in. If you have some time to speak about your experience there, I'd love to ask you some questions.
Best, Arun

This message accomplishes a couple things:

- It gives Sandy a compelling reason to speak with me, as I may turn in to a referral that will make him look good.
- It is brief and easy to understand. If Sandy gets a lot of messages each day, this gives him everything he needs in a message that fits into LinkedIn's 300 character limit (including paragraph spaces).

Advanced search function

In my opinion, the most effective means of finding people on LinkedIn is the advanced people search function. In LinkedIn's current design, click in the top search bar, then click "People," then just beneath the search bar click "all filters." From there you have everything you should need to find people who could be valuable connections. Go into your LinkedIn settings and change your profile viewing settings to private mode. This enables you to view other peoples' profiles without them knowing that you viewed them.

There are a few fields that are important to search to find people who will help you:
- Title (keyword)

- Current company
- School
- Location
- Connections

Try to find people with whom you have shared a piece of your career or have a mutual connection (2nd degree connections). Perhaps you went to the same school or worked for the same company. Familiarity of any kind immediately gives you a better chance of a response. If you know what company you want to learn more about, filter by current company. If you know a title that interests you based on a job description you read, find 2nd degree connections with that title. If you want to move cities, find people who worked at your current company or alumni from your school in that city.

You may be able to ask a mutual connection to introduce you. Depending on the relationship you have with your mutual connection and the relationship that person has with the 2nd degree connection, this tactic may be an easy way for you to get connected. That request will vary depending on how close you are to your connection, but could look like any of these:

- Over text message: Hey, I see you know Debbie on LinkedIn, would you be willing to introduce me? I think she'd be a great person to talk to about her career in investment banking.
- Over email: Hello Alexa, hope you're doing well. I see you're connected with Sean on LinkedIn. How did you meet him? If you're open to it, I would really appreciate an introduction. He is doing some amazing work with artificial intelligence and I would love to support him with my background in HR.
- Over LinkedIn: Hello Fredrick, we met at South by Southwest last year. I see you've since moved to Apple from Cisco - have you enjoyed the change? I'm reaching out because I see you're connected with Kylie, the SVP at Pepsi. I know their CEO has been trying to integrate healthier products into their portfolio, and I think I could benefit the company's goals with my Corporate Development experience. If you're comfortable, do you think you could introduce us?

None of these methods is guaranteed to work, and you may ultimately have to take the first step towards making a new connection yourself. Nevertheless, introductions are better received than a cold connection.

Your Profile

When reaching out, you will want your connection request recipient to respond positively to your profile. There is already plenty of guidance out there on creating the perfect LinkedIn profile that you can use. The following advice is just my opinions, tried and tested by myself and deemed a successful format for your profile.

Your profile should be two things: easy to understand and unique. I do not care who you are, you have life experience, work experience, and a background that you can put forth to make your profile (and therefore you as a potential connection) unique. You also are using LinkedIn for a very clear purpose. There should be no ambiguity that you are reaching out to folks to learn more about their profession as you go through your career eager to make an impact on the professional world.

Here are just a few pieces of advice based on what I think is the most effective way to portray yourself through your profile:

- Use a professional profile photo. Go outside, find a nice background, and have someone with portrait mode on their phone take a picture of you from the chest up.
- You do not have to fill out every section, but completely fill out education and experience.
- Your headline should be your job title, if you have one, as well as your major and school, if you're in college (i.e. Credit Analyst at Presidio Bank | Accounting major at Santa Clara University). I do not believe in putting something like "seeking opportunities in accounting." You do not need it and it subordinates you to your potential connections.
- Your summary should be in the form of (i) here is who I am; (ii) here is why I am on LinkedIn; and (iii) here is

what I am doing. Here is my example from while I was writing this book:

I inspire and equip young professionals to build their ideal careers.

I also work with automotive business owners to create and execute strategic projects.

Want to connect? Please include a note if we do not know each other personally.

--Career Coaching--

Are you a college student or young professional, and:
- Looking at the perfect job, but not 100% confident in your application?
- Feeling stuck in your job, but need help finding a new, exciting role?
- Out of work or internship rescinded due to the ongoing pandemic?

I'm your guy. I can help you define your dream career and get the jobs to fulfill it.

You can send me an email at arun@findprofessionalsuccess.com to book a free 30 minute consultation! I am also offering steep discounts to those whose jobs have been affected by COVID-19.

My book, Professional Success - the Career Building Blueprint, which gives you the tools to begin building your ideal career, comes out in May 2020! Visit findprofessionalsuccess.com/book to learn more.

--Automotive Strategy--

I help automotive businesses to design and implement strategic growth and change projects. I am currently a consultant to Wrench Studios, a garage specializing in car performance and aesthetic modification, and Electric GT, an electric production car racing series.

--Education--

Starting this summer, I will be attending London Business School for my MBA, class of 2022. I graduated Magna Cum Laude from Santa Clara University in 2017.

When I was in college, my summary looked like this:

I am an Accounting Major at Santa Clara University, expecting to graduate in March 2017. I intend to start working full time for PwC in their capital markets and accounting advisory practice after passing the CPA in the summer.

I am involved in a variety of extracurriculars with the aim of developing my professional knowledge and my network. I am Senior Officer of the SCU Accounting Association, and VP of Finance for Alpha Kappa Psi, a professional business fraternity.

I am currently working as an analyst with Harvest Management Partners, a boutique investment banking focused on the automotive and technology sectors. I am also working part time as an assistant to the club finance director for SCU.

I am interested in learning more about M&A consulting and part-time work opportunities for summer 2017. You may hear from me regarding one of these topics.

Check out my LinkedIn profile to get more ideas. Send me a message and connection request!

Author's note: LinkedIn Premium

LinkedIn Premium is very expensive. The primary benefits I see in buying it are:
- Unlimited searches. Without premium, you will be restricted to 3 results per search after using up the initial search limit.
- You can see who viewed your profile even while your own settings are set to private mode.

My response to these points?

For $40+ per month, these benefits are not good value for money. I could be missing the benefits of many features, but I am able to do everything I need without Premium.

- Make your searches very specific and you can get the people you need into the first 3 results.

- You don't need to know who viewed your profile. You probably already viewed their profile.

Step 5: Plan your Path

Careers are a jungle gym, not a ladder. Ladders are limiting—people can move up or down, on or off. Jungle gyms offer more creative exploration. There's only one way to get to the top of a ladder, but there are many ways to get to the top of a jungle gym.

- Sheryl Sandberg

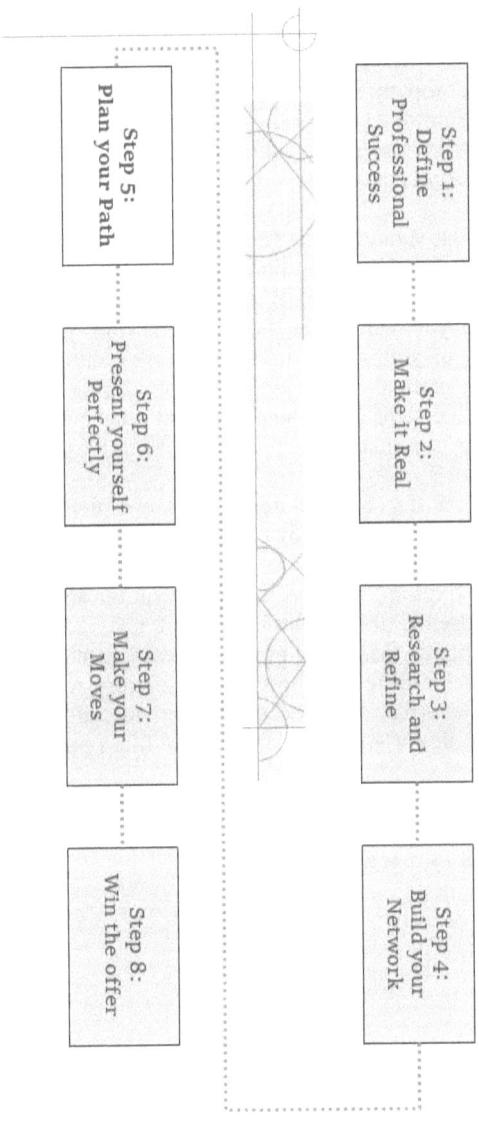

You will have learned the following from your research thus far:

- Expected compensation in your potential paths
- Company culture of companies on your potential paths
- Employee reviews via interviews of potential paths
- A first-person account of what it is like to work at your target companies

Your list should be narrowed down to no more than 2 or 3 potential paths. They may be very similar in nature; they may be very different. The diversity of your potential paths will dictate how wide you will leave the door open for yourself to travel down any of your paths (i.e., how much commitment you take towards a particular path while still exploring others). As you complete the steps listed below, revisit your potential paths and continue to eliminate.

The first step of your research is complete. Now you can begin to plan and move down the path to your next job based on what you have learned so far. I call this step exploratory research. Exploratory research is education and experience in your fields and roles of interest that take you towards your potential paths. Education and experience come in many forms. As you tackle different forms of exploratory research, you will accumulate skills, experiences, and qualifications that create a strong profile for you as a candidate for those potential paths.

This step looks very different depending on whether you are in college or whether you have already begun your career. I have broken out each scenario separately.

Exploratory research - college students

Change your major: I went into college intending to declare a major in political science on my pre-law track. After one term (to get a head start, I enrolled in three political science classes), I learned I was not at all interested in a career in political science. I found the theory behind politics to be even more dry than politics itself and realized that studying government was not as appealing as the law-based TV shows I watched as a kid.

I needed to take a step back and think about what educational direction I wanted to go in before diving back into a single major with both feet. I took microeconomics during my second term as a required class in my college's core curriculum. Something about supply and demand curves made sense to me, with massive clarity relative to the topics of my political philosophy class. I was given the opportunity to apply for a transfer to the business school at my college, and I was accepted. I went on to take the "Introduction to Business Concepts" course, where I was exposed to a high-level understanding of each of the business majors on offer at my college. Accounting clicked in my head. I understood it intuitively. No other section of the course gave me the same satisfaction of success.

I came back my sophomore year with the idea to declare my major in accounting. I enrolled in the introduction to financial accounting class. In the first class of the year, I confirmed that accounting still made sense to me intuitively. I walked straight from that first class to the program office and declared my major in accounting. The last five and a half years since declaring my major have brought me plenty of academic and career success, which I attribute in part to an intuitive understanding of accounting.

Change your school: A friend of mine in college was a marketing major during her sophomore year. We went to a university known primarily for its business school and connections in the accounting and tech industries based in the area. She was pursuing an art minor on the side, but finding her studies challenging as she focused more and more on her art minor, disengaged from her accounting and economics classes required as part of the mandatory core of the business school. Near the end of sophomore year, she announced that she was pursuing a transfer to a different university, which was renowned for its art program. She got the transfer, thrived in her new university taking predominantly art classes and participating in the graphic design club, and now works as a production designer, on her path to Professional Success.

Get an internship: The summer between my freshman and sophomore year of school was miserable. I could not get a job that moved my career forward at all, because I had no relevant education or experience. I ended up working at a nursing home, painting the walls, and helping residents move in. I went back to school sophomore year determined to get work experience related to my new accounting major and income.

Now that I had some direction with a declared major in accounting, I was able to focus my search. Over the next three years, I worked in seven jobs spanning four and a half years' worth of part-time experience (I overlapped part time jobs, working in multiple at a time). Each of these positions taught me about the company, the industry, and the job function in a way I could never have learned from an informational interview. Internships are a low-commitment undertaking. Sure, you have a very limited amount of time in college to take on summer internships, but there is nothing stopping you from taking on an internship or two at a time during the school year as well. For a one-month period at the beginning of my junior year, I was taking five classes and working three jobs. It was unsustainable, but through communication and excessive planning, I was able to make it work temporarily. All for the sake of more experience.

I got my internships mostly through the same sort of tactics described in this book. Four positions I was offered through a referral from either a classmate leaving the job or a professor who knew of the job opening. The other three I was offered through my own networking and good timing. While I may have interviewed somewhere in the process for some of the larger, more structured internships, I interviewed directly for only two of those seven internships. The others I was offered based on my presentation during the networking process. More about that in Step 6.

Join or start a club: College clubs are a great way to get experience in leadership and basic technical skills. Many often lead to jobs, professional development, skill building, and are great for your resume.

I was Senior Officer of the Accounting Association, VP of Finance for my business fraternity, and briefly the co-founder of the Investment Banking Club at Santa Clara University. Each of these experiences showed up on my resume and gave me experience with corporate sponsorships, executive committee meetings, bad morale, leadership, recruiting, event planning, and treasury responsibilities. I was able to learn a ton from these positions where I was given more responsibility and leadership than a traditional internship.

Case competitions and hackathons: Case competitions and hackathons are great ways to set yourself apart from your peers and gain valuable experience that you can talk about in an interview and put on your resume.

When I interviewed for my first real finance job, my second-round interviewer was unimpressed with my resume and my answers to her initial questions. I could tell from her body language that I was not giving her the impression that I was the right fit for the job. Near the end of the interview, she asked me to describe a recent success story. The week before, I had come in second place in a business strategy case competition on a team formed at the information session for the event. We did not know each other and were not friends, and it ended up being an advantage. We all wanted to learn, win, and stay accountable to our teammates. I was very surprised that we ended up coming in second. When I told this story to my interviewer, she was impressed at what I had been able to learn from the case competition and went on to ask me more questions about it, giving me a chance to shine through the experience. I received the job offer the following week.

Shadow: You may be able to find someone who will offer to let you shadow them. This experience will help you understand what it really looks like to work in certain full-time roles. Take note of the work environment, ask more detailed questions about specific tasks, try to understand whether the little window of time in which you are shadowing represents a typical or an atypical working day. Ideally, you will be invited to shadow a few different people within the same industry or company. You can ask to shadow someone once you have built a stronger rapport with that person and you are confident you will not be violating any confidentiality issues.

I was once invited for a brief shadow and a lunch with the audit team from one of the Big Four accounting firms serving one of their most prestigious, big name clients. I went to visit the team in March, about a month after their "busy season" had ended.

There were ten people packed into a small room arranged in one big square desk, all along the wall of the room. In the corner, there was a table covered with instant noodles and Cheetos. I did not foresee anyone from the client visiting this room to get strategic accounting advice or help executing the next transaction. I saw a meat grinder. *(Disclaimer: I never worked in audit, but I have several friends who do work in audit. Not every audit room is like this.)*

I learned that while the accounting firm put this prestigious client's logo on their recruiting presentations, that did not mean that working on that client would be prestigious, glamorous, or career-developing in an area of my interest. Shadowing allowed me to peek behind the curtain to see that.

Create your own internship: Sometimes you have to create your own opportunity to do exploratory research.

My first "internship" was a role I scored through luck. Despite no prior experience and one accounting class under my belt, an Executive Vice President of a small, Bay Area bank serving high net worth individuals took a chance with me based on a single email I wrote to him after he promoted a generic opening at his bank. He played golf in college and graduated with a sub-3.0 GPA, and I was on Team A of my university's ultimate frisbee team, traveling to tournaments with the team on the weekends and not particularly focused on my career development or coursework. He hired me because he liked athletes, even though there were better qualified candidates from more prestigious schools nearby.

I was hired as a part-time credit analyst working 15 hours per week. I spent a year there, learning and helping the bank grow by taking on all the low-level work I could. There was only one task assigned to me when I started, and over time I learned higher level activities and began to understand more about how the bank operated and how I could best contribute. I took note of this progression over the course of my year of working there. When it was time for me to leave, as my coursework got harder and I started working other jobs closer to campus, I hired my own replacement. I designed a structured internship for students who were in the same position I was in to learn about office culture, retail banking, and finance and accounting (I learned how to read a tax return from that job, not from my tax class. The internship continues today, giving early-college students the chance to learn those valuable skills at a time when they are still exploring their potential paths.

This opportunity can present itself in many ways. I encourage you to reach out to companies to offer yourself as an intern before a job opportunity even presents itself.

Exploratory research - working professionals

Do a bootcamp: I know at least half a dozen computer engineers who broke into the profession through a coding bootcamp. They spent a week or a month learning how to code. They took their skills forward and continued learning with self-motivated study, eventually building the confidence to pass a technical interview. Similar bootcamps exist in the world of finance and consulting and could be worth the investment if you find yourself a bit behind the learning curve. If you know with a fair amount of certainty that doing the bootcamp would point you in the right direction, go for it.

During my junior year, I signed up for a $100 course called "Wall Street Prep - Financial Modeling." The course spanned 12 hours between a Saturday and a Sunday, and I had a couple of friends with whom I was signed up for the course. I overslept on Saturday and missed most of the first day's worth of training. I went to the second day, got the half-completed financial model from a friend, and finished the course without feeling like I learned much of anything, not really enjoying myself in the process.

This experience taught me two things: first, considering I overslept and missed most of the first day, I clearly had not acknowledged how I felt towards a career in finance. While it sounded glamorous, I lacked the motivation to get up with my alarm and make it to day 1. Second, although the financial model we built was complex, I struggled to draw the line from the financial model to its real-world application and impact. I was not interested in the work it would take to learn how that line was drawn, and I didn't consider myself a born financial modeler (unlike some Excel-ninjas I now have the pleasure of knowing). In other words, I was not very skilled in financial modeling either. This bootcamp taught me what not to do.

Leverage your network: If you are further along in your career, chances are you have built a strong network that is supportive of your success by way of working with you and appreciating you as a person. As I address in Step 4 and Step 8, who you know is often the make-or-break component of a successful job search. It is easy to meet and get to know people, it is hard to understand just how powerful that resource can be.

In my move to London, I had the opportunity to interview with a strategy consulting firm for a position in London, set to begin soon after I moved. I got the opportunity without applying to a position. A friend of mine from college had worked for this firm for 3 years. I reached out to him to let him know I was interested in working for his firm and asked if we could talk about his experience. In a 20-minute conversation I was able to learn so much more about the internal organization of the firm than I ever would have from Google. Further, he offered to refer me. Referral bonus for him, new job for me.

Over the next two weeks, he vouched for me to the extent that he was essentially interviewing on my behalf. We spoke several more times for him to understand my motivations, personal situation, and qualifications. He was an extremely strong advocate, following up with the hiring team and pushing me through the internal process. Ultimately, I chose to pursue an MBA rather than push harder on a very slow hiring decision process, but the example stands - it's who you know. Networks are powerful.

Internal moves: Perhaps a potential path for you is within your current company. Internal moves can be politically tricky, but also can be easy to execute. The biggest two factors are articulating a compelling story (see Step 6) and building strong relationships with your current colleagues. The most prevalent fears people experience when considering an internal job change relate to breaching the conversation and offending their current team. If you have a compelling story and strong relationships with your team, this will not be an issue. Your team will be sad, as they will be losing someone who is a strong contributor and teammate, but they will want what is best for you and support you however they can. Step 6 describes how to create a story. Once you have a story, set up a time to talk with your manager.

In that conversation, introduce your story. You are compelled to make a greater impact working on something that matters to you deeply. You think you will use your strongest skills more and you are excited by what that other team is doing. With the manager's support, you think you have a better chance of successfully making the change.

If you have a strong relationship with your manager, they will react positively to you being upfront and transparent. Do not go behind your team's back to try to get the job. This is almost guaranteed to void any chance you have of getting the job, as your manager will learn about your actions from the new team that you have applied to when asked for a reference.

My internal move story starts with getting married and my wife moving to London. I started the conversation with my manager as soon as I contemplated the decision of moving and laid out my story. My story in this case did involve personal reasons, but there were also a variety of professional reasons that a move to London made sense for both me and the company. I got several introductions to people working in my group in London, learned that people in London reached out for references to people in the US, and had a job offer within 3 months of starting the conversation, without even interviewing. This was a product of a few things: first, I had a compelling story as to why moving would be beneficial for myself and the company; second, I built great relationships with my managers in the US; and third, I worked for a global organization, which I picked partly for the ability to work internationally.

Entrepreneurship: If you are not able to find a company solving problems that you care about, create the company.

Entrepreneurship has been blown up into a sexy, special pursuit that everyone can do, if they just grind hard enough. In reality, entrepreneurship does not mean you must work 16-hour days, 7 days a week. Do not let the reputation of long hours and their consequences put you off. Entrepreneurship can take many different forms. No step is too small to start. Test the waters and monitor your satisfaction and impact very, very closely.

While there are consulting firms focused on the automotive industry, the automotive aftermarket performance and modification space does not have any sort of strategy leadership. I want a secure job after my MBA, but I also know what I really want to do. There appears to be an unfulfilled need for help with strategy development and execution in the automotive aftermarket. I created my own automotive aftermarket strategy consulting firm and work on it each day with excitement and commitment.

Go back to school: The most effective means of qualifying yourself for a new job is to get a degree or certification related to that field. Certifications of various kinds often open new doors to different career paths. Some examples include: real estate agent, certified financial planner, *career coach,* construction tradespeople, and many more. Certifications and licenses may have a lower barrier to entry than a full master's degree and enable a faster job transition.

The time you spend getting a postgraduate degree represents an opportunity for you to explore using many of the methods listed in the previous student section. If you can afford it and it makes sense to seek out given your life circumstances, then it could be a worthwhile investment. If it would be burdensome and otherwise difficult to go back to school, do not consider this path until you have exhausted all other options.

I met with one of my former college professors prior to moving to London, at a time when I was exploring a move into strategy consulting, where I believed I would find greater job satisfaction through Trait 3 - I'd care more about the impact I was making. He told me that in order to be successful as a strategy consultant, I would need to get an MBA from a reputable school. I also bought a book about case interviews – business-centric technical interviews that you must pass in order to get an offer from any consulting firm – and began studying. I found very quickly that there was a lot I needed to learn about business strategy, and that I would need to go through a massive amount of self-study in order to feel confident for a case interview. Alternatively, I could get an MBA, which would better qualify me for consulting, and give me all the resources I need to pass the case interview. Upon doing the research, I learned that one of the MBA programs best suited to strategy consultant post-MBA careers was London Business School's program, where, conveniently, my wife was starting in a couple months' time. I applied, wrote an application essay about how I wanted to apply strategy to my love of cars (Traits 1, 2, and 3) and was accepted. Using my future-MBA brand, I have started my own strategy consulting firm and began conversations with multiple automotive consulting firms, setting my career transition in motion before I even begin the MBA.

As you can see, there are a variety of options available to you for exploring your potential paths, with various levels of commitment. After completing this exploratory research, you should have **one** job or path in mind that will serve as your first step towards Professional Success. You will have accumulated additional qualifications and experiences to help you build your profile as a strong candidate for this job. You will have started down your path.

You should know from your research what additional qualifications you likely need to present yourself as the perfect candidate for your target job. Plan out the rest of your path to get there. Create several steps, as needed, to ensure you are building your network, getting your certifications, and then presenting yourself perfectly to get the job.

It is up to you to go execute. You must present yourself as someone who believes they are on the path of Professional Success. This is where the satisfaction and engagement are guaranteed.

Step 6: Present yourself Perfectly

A good first impression can work wonders.

- J.K. Rowling

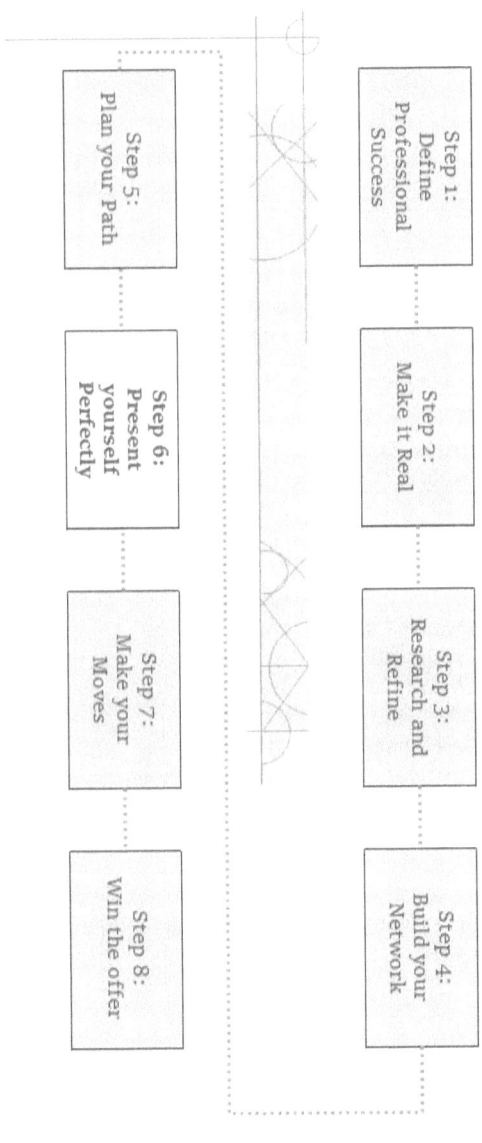

Step 1: Define Professional Success

Step 2: Make it Real

Step 3: Research and Refine

Step 4: Build your Network

Step 5: Plan your Path

Step 6: Present yourself Perfectly

Step 7: Make your Moves

Step 8: Win the offer

You will earn each step along the path you just designed by presenting yourself in a well thought out, precise manner to the gatekeepers of your next step.

Resumes

I believe the most important aspect of a resume to consider is always the audience.

Your resume will serve a variety of purposes in your career. At this stage, the first question you must ask yourself when building your resume is "what purpose is this serving for me?" Think about the following:
-   Who will be reading your resume?
-   What is that person looking to learn about you from that resume?
-   What do you want that person you learn about you from your resume?

A few examples are:
-   A new informational interview contact is reading your resume upon their request after your initial conversation. You want them to learn about your experience and how it could contribute to your connection's business.
-   A scholarship board is reviewing your resume as part of your application for their scholarship. You want them to understand that you are a dedicated student who is making an impact in their community.
-   A professor has asked for your resume to pass along to a contact of theirs for a potential part-time job opportunity you asked about previously. You want to convey to your professor and the contact that you would be a great addition to the team.

If I were making each of these resumes for myself, they would all look slightly different. I would tweak the language in the bullet points, the arrangement of different sections and jobs, and the format to accomplish each goal I am shooting for.

LinkedIn

Read the subchapter on LinkedIn for my thoughts on creating a strong LinkedIn profile.

Check out my LinkedIn profile to get some ideas. Send me a message and connection request!

Your story

Knowing your story is a very important part of presenting yourself to others as you move along your path toward Professional Success. Your story is very simple - you must answer a single question: why are you here?

"Why are you here" is the generic version of this question. In reality, it comes in a few different forms. On LinkedIn, the question is "why are you reaching out to me on LinkedIn?" In an informational interview, the question is "why do you want to talk to me?" In a real interview, the question is "why are you sitting in that chair, seeking out this job?"

Your answer should take no more than sixty seconds. It should come naturally. Do not rehearse a script. What I do is take five minutes before walking into a conversation where I will have to present my story, to consider why I am there. If you are truly moving along your path toward Professional Success, this should come very easily. My story, these days, is one of two:

- I am here to understand my market for career coaching and how to reach them.
- I am here to learn about your automotive business and offer you strategic solutions to your problems.

I am very clear and well-practiced on these stories from telling them in real-world situations. I add in context based on the audience. For example:

- I am here to learn about your performance car parts business and your experience with being an owner. I find myself compelled to help automotive business owners retain their passion for cars and do so through working with those owners to understand changes that would benefit their business. From that understanding we can design and execute strategic projects that will help you return to growth, something that I've noticed has faltered in recent years.

As a student, my story sounded more like this:

- I declared my accounting major on the first day of sophomore year because it was the business subject that just clicked for me. I find that accounting comes pretty easily to me compared to other subjects, and I would love the opportunity to explore its practical application in the business world through a summer internship. I applied specifically to the internship at your firm because I met some of your staff at a recent networking event and heard great things about the working culture and leadership.

These stories should be presented at the beginning of your conversations. They set the stage for targeted, direct, and efficient chats that provide the other person with plenty of information to work with in terms of who you are, what you want from speaking to the other person, and what the other person can get out of the conversation. Be assertive about telling your story at the outset. Continue to develop them with each iteration of the same conversation. Look for reaction cues from the other person. A vocal or facial acknowledgement of being impressed, curious, or happy indicate that you should use whatever you just said in your next story.

Physical Presentation

Your attire and your overall physical presentation are a major component of every in-person and video meeting. The one principle I recommend you follow is this: Be confident in yourself. Whatever you are wearing, whatever your hair looks like, whether you are wearing makeup or accessories or whatever else to make yourself look professional, leave the house confident in yourself after looking in the mirror. Your clothes should be as close to perfect as you can get them. Use the company website and/or ask your network to figure out what the appropriate level of formality is for your attire.

Smile. Have a firm handshake if meeting in person. Sit upright, make eye contact, and relax. Remember that the person across from you is still a person. They were once in your shoes. They understand the nerves and will be impressed by you if you are relaxed, confident, and well-presented.

You should be confident in your story, confident in the way you presented yourself through your resume or LinkedIn, and confident in how you look. You are working toward Professional Success. You are the perfect person for the job, or you are doing necessary research to determine if you are the perfect person for the job. If you articulate this clearly, the person on the other end hears it and understands it, and they are compelled to help you in return for facilitating career satisfaction, productivity, employee engagement, and overall economic success for their business, you are doing everything right.

Send a follow up email, as discussed previously for informational interviews.

Step 7: Make your Moves

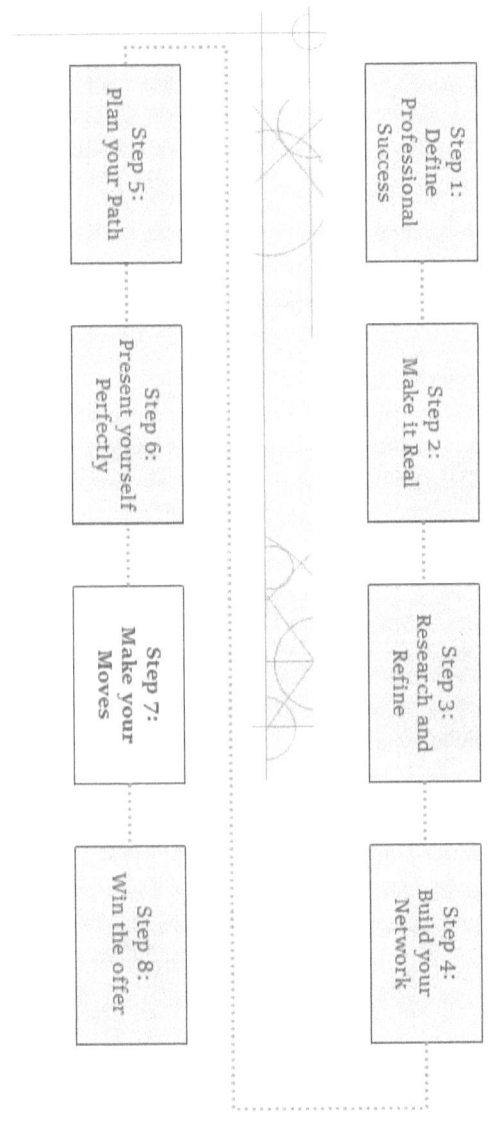

This chapter marks the time for you to execute, giving you a high-level view of the whole blueprint. Making your career building moves could look something like this:

Create a step-by-step plan for yourself based on your definition of Professional Success. Build up your qualifications, knowledge, and relevant experience, that will lead you towards ideal positions at ideal companies earning your ideal life, where you're working on projects you're passionate about, that interest you, and that allow you to use your strongest skills. (Steps 1-3)

Make a cold LinkedIn connection request to someone whose career you admire and ask them if you could speak with them about it (Step 4). Get the training, position yourself in the school and major best suited for you, attend a bootcamp to get the basics quickly (Step 5). They may be impressed by you and your conviction. They may say "there is someone you should talk to in X company, which is very similar to ours." You will get a second informational interview by referral. Now you have two connections you can reach out to for advice, provided you have presented yourself well and made a good impression (Step 6). You may have learned that while the job interests you, the expectation of weekly working hours is too high. You find someone else on LinkedIn with a slightly different title but who appears to work in the same industry. They work at a different company. You research the company and find its values are more employee-centric. You know a friend of your Aunt used to work there. You get hold of the friend and ask a few questions. This seems like a better fit for your next job. You prepare your presentation (Step 6) and make your pitch to your connection (Step 8) on the path toward Professional Success.

You have landed on a single path that you are going to pursue. You know who the ideal candidate is that they are looking for. Are you presenting yourself as that person? Have you done all you could to increase your chances? Have you made it known you are considering that role to the relevant people? Create a plan that will help you answer each of these questions as a yes, like the above story.

Now that you know what role you are pursuing and prepared yourself to pursue it, set yourself up for success. Use pieces of the next chapter in executing your plan in the best way possible.

Step 8: Win the Offer

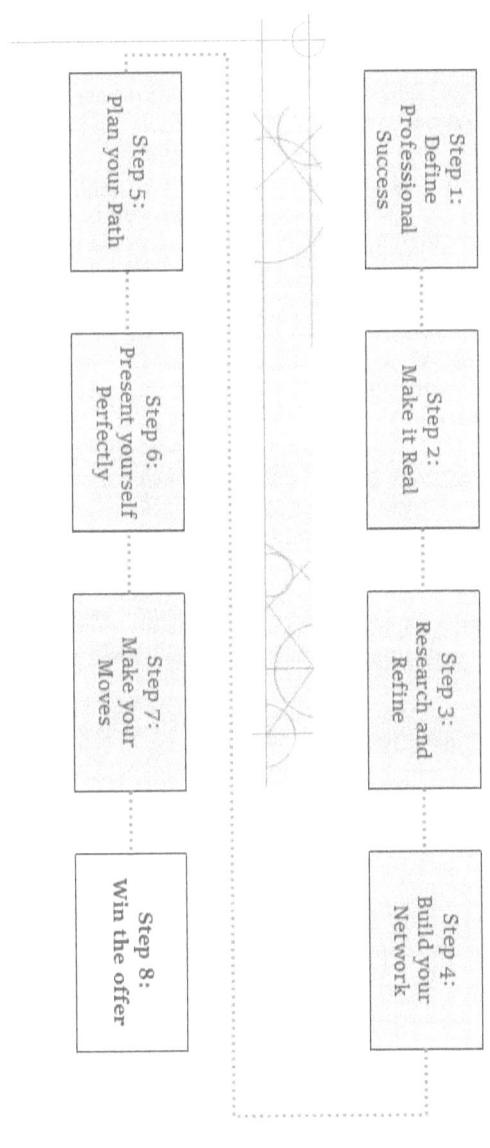

You may have already gotten your full-time offer for your next job and are confident in the research you have done and the steps you have taken. You are well on your way to Professional Success. However, if you have built a strong network and are awaiting that final offer, you are getting prepared to make your change. You need to execute to get the job.

You will have made some connections with people who are close to that job, whether they are in the same company or in the same function. You will have made a good impression on them based on your enthusiasm, confidence, and intentionality. Using this lasting impression, you will now reach out to them with a slightly different question. Where before you were looking for information, now you are looking for opportunities. **This method should only be used when the company hires off-cycle, instead of solely through a formal, standardized recruiting cycle for your target next job.** If they follow a standardized recruiting process, you must follow procedure. Do all you can outside of that procedure to increase your odds, such as getting a referral and building your network with interviewers and decision makers.

Send all your relevant connections an email or a LinkedIn message. Tailor the formality of the message, but ask this question:

"I am currently open to opportunities in X (describe aspects of your Professional Success), and I am wondering if you know of any current or upcoming openings in X (describe the group, role, or function)."

You are not asking this individual to find you a job or float your resume through to the hiring decision maker. This easy task has a much lower barrier to execute than your contact putting themselves out there for your reputation.

The timing of this message matters. You want to ensure you are getting in touch with your connection around the time you are expecting those opportunities to be available. If you are aiming for a role that has a predictable recruiting and hiring cycle, then you should easily time your message. In this situation, make sure you are writing to someone who can actually make the decision, as opposed to a recruiter who told you about that cycle to begin with. They might have a bit of impact on a final hiring decision, but their job is getting quality candidates through the door, not deciding who is the perfect fit for the group for which they are recruiting.

If you do not hear back, follow up. This practice applies to all areas of communication. Once you have made a connection, you know that that person is willing to be of even a small amount of help. People respect persistence. Remember, you are following your Professional Success and you are clear on your motivations. This confidence should enable you to authentically follow up with your connection in a respectful, polite, and understanding manner. There are any number of reasons why you have not heard back. Do not assume the worst. Read Step 4 to learn more about following up.

The response will be one of the following:
-    No, there are no openings
-    Yes, let me point you to our online job posting
-    Yes, let me directly refer you to that job
-    Yes, let me introduce you to the person who is hiring

If the answer is no, be patient. Continue your research, expand your list, explore more options, and consider whether an opportunity may arise for that particular job in the future.

If you are pointed to an online job posting, respond and ask your connection whether they would be comfortable introducing you to the owner of the job posting. If the answer is no, ask if your connection would be comfortable with you using their name to reach out to some additional people at the company. If the answer is no, revisit Steps 4 and 5, along with the LinkedIn subchapter.

If you are referred directly to the job, your chances are improving. Ask your connection if they would be comfortable introducing you to the owner of the job posting and providing a written endorsement. If no, ask if your connection would be comfortable with you using their name to reach out. If no, you can still reach out to additional contacts at your target company and include in your message "I have been referred to X job and would appreciate the chance to discuss my qualifications."

If you are introduced to the hiring decision maker, you are well on your way to getting the job. Perform in the interview, tell your story, flex your skills, demonstrate your interest, and await the offer.

Conclusion

This program works for anyone at any stage of their career. What you are asking of yourself is a better career trajectory of satisfaction, fulfillment, engagement, and impact. What you are doing to satisfy that request is research, intentional action, and relying on others to respect and understand your conviction.

After reading this book, you will hopefully place yourself - and keep yourself - on the path toward your Professional Success. **Revisit your definition often, once a year at least, to determine if your life and your job still align to your Professional Success and assess whether your definition is still appropriate for you.**

Your path towards Professional Success will never be perfect. I believe, however, that approaching your career through this method will maximize satisfaction, engagement, and impact.

If you want more hands-on coaching for transitioning your career into Professional Success, I offer coaching to provide tailored, personal advice to you in your present situation. I will work with you in defining your Professional Success, helping you to design your step-by-step plan, conduct research, present yourself, and win the job.

Visit findprofessionalsuccess.com to learn more.

If you find any aspects of this program fall short of success for you, please get in touch and we can work together to see where it can be improved and help you win the role that will set you on the path towards Professional Success.

I would love to hear how the blueprint helps you on your path to Professional Success.

Resources

Resumes and LinkedIn: cultivatedculture.com

Attire and Presentation: Executive Presence by Sylvia Ann Hewlett

Earning the Life you Want: Lifestyle Costing by Tim Ferriss: tim.blog/lifestyle-costing

Networking: Never Eat Alone by Keith Ferrazi

Financial Planning: Unshakeable by Tony Robbins